ELIZABETH L. AUDU

THE EMPTY CHAMBER OUT OF THE EPHEMERAL THING

Portraying the Frailty of Humanity

By the same author:

Approved by God?
The Narrow Gate

Mereo Books

2nd Floor, 6-8 Dyer Street, Cirencester, Gloucestershire, GL7 2PF
An imprint of Memoirs Books. www.mereobooks.com
and www.memoirsbooks.co.uk

THE EMPTY CHAMBER OUT OF THE EPHEMERAL THING

First published in Great Britain in 2022
by Mereo Books, an imprint of Memoirs Books.

The address for Memoirs Books can be
found at www.mereobooks.com

Mereo Books Ltd. Reg. No. 12157152

Typeset in 12/18pt Century Schoolbook
by Wiltshire Associates.
Printed and bound in Great Britain

Introduction

The human heart is an organ within a chamber, regulated by the oxygen in the system, but when it ceases to function the entire human body is more or less like that of any other mammal. You and I are better off because we were created with a sense of humour, able to communicate, to acknowledge right from wrong doing, and know what necessary action that needs to be taken into consideration in case of any concerns.

The ephemeral thing is worldly affairs or activities that are solely meant for a certain limited period of time. They do not last long.

This manuscript came into being due to the Word of Knowledge and was penned as divinely instructed. It will be illustrated through secular and spiritual writing. Please realise that humanity is made of the spirit, soul and body. They are intertwined within the system and utilised for our daily living.

I happened to work as a carer within the hospital ward environment in the United Kingdom. On one particular day, while I resumed my routine shift, which was a scheduled late shift. I was warmly welcomed by the nurse in charge and members of the team, but noticed one of the bedside curtains was drawn. To my surprise, the name of the charge nurse (male) is still fresh in my memory, but due to data protection and confidentialities names are withheld.

He was a passionate nurse whom I will never forget. All interpersonal skills applied to him. He calmed me down. I sat by the bedside of the patient, who had just passed away. I had no clue of what, when, how it happened, or was handed over any information. Meanwhile, I was jittering, panicking, and even decided to pick up my bag and go off to my house. I was offered a cup of tea, and felt a bit relaxed. The only sentence that came out of the nurse's mouth was: "Why are you scared? This person is just an empty chamber. He cannot hurt nor do anyone any harm".

I couldn't respond to his statement. The only assignment he allocated to me was to remove a ring from the deceased's finger. This was a frightening task and a reflective moment for me. He never realised until later that I had had such a traumatic life experience at an early stage in my life.

As I was writing this manuscript, it was on that day, 27th of May 2021, that the Lord reminded me of this book, because one thing led to another. I would have written it, but unforeseen circumstances, time factors and unnecessary procrastinations are not reasons not to execute God's instruction or purpose driven assignment. As you are reading it, may you be blessed and achieve the rationale of this awakening piece of manuscript.

Do you realise that when people have some life experiences there could be traumatised circumstances reflecting through their emotional, psychological, physical, financial and marital lives and could affect their lifestyles? On that note, it is paramount to raise the awareness on health and well-being of the individual within the family, community, even at a national level that have gone through diverse life events such as bereavement, natural disasters, terminal illness, sickness, an epidemic or war.

The notion behind the writing of this book is

that people have not learned the lessons of the Covid-19 pandemic. I had the opportunity by the special grace of God to travel with a reputable group of people on a missionary journey to attend a meeting of clergy at New York in 2019. We lodged in one of the prestigious hotels with dignitaries from all over the globe who gathered together in unity and love. We had a great time in the presence of the Lord. In the twinkling of an eye, one week after our arrival back to our individual locations came the news of the newly-emerged deadly virus of Covid-19, which made the news headlines 24/7. The irony of it was that people were dying within seconds and minutes on a daily basis, and the situation was disheartening. Thereafter divinely, the way forward towards the invention of vaccines through scientific research came into the limelight with positive outcomes for the benefits of lives being saved all over the world. Although, some people have forgotten too soon that they are spared to be alive by God's special grace, not by their strength, nor by waging war against one another.

This piece of work is to raise the awareness that you came to this Earth with nothing and will exit with nothing. All accumulated wealth is temporary and vanity. Hence, your existence on earth is paramount. You are created or born for a purpose, to impact the world. May I suggest please, let's show someone love and kindness in accordance with God's agenda. It is a commandment, as HE did this for humanity, showing kindness, supporting without segregation or discrimination. God created the whole universe, He is God of all flesh, there should be no disunity between fellow brother or sister. Whether you are Christian, Muslim, Judaist, Hindus, atheist, even an unbeliever, He owns the whole world. He cares for all humanity, and expects you to be a helper of destiny. Great Britain, the United States of America, Canada, France and other Western countries are able to show compassion to other parts of the world. Let us all endeavour to emulate that way of life. The LORD is doing good to mankind created in His own image. You also can do likewise. ***(John 3:16): For God so loved the world, He gave His only begotten Son, that whosoever believeth in him should not perish, but have everlasting life.***

Whatsoever you do unto your next person, either neighbour, colleague, friend, family, community in the market place, on air, land, or sea, you do all unto God for a Heavenly Kingdom reward.

As I was instructed to pen this piece of information, I implore you to please strive to help someone. As we all are sojourners on this planet, all the accumulated materialism is left behind at the end of time. It isn't worth unnecessary unrest. Therefore, the ***Empty Chamber out of the Ephemeral Thing that portrayed the frailty of mankind is a wake-up manuscript to raise awareness of good role model and positive legacy against materialism that ends in Vain glory. Thus: demonstration of someone that travelled on a journey, definitely you must go back home. No matter how long you spent on earth, you must exit someday. Nevertheless, when the oxygenated system is impaired one becomes vulnerable, frail, and dependable. Hence, you will go back to give account how you have traded on earth. This signifies how one comes to the realisation of owing nothing, existing*** *under borrowed time. As the struggles of life continues (All is Vanity).*

God has given the opportunity of the (Time and Chance) to impact your world, according to the account of *(Ecclesiastes 9:10-11) :*

10 *Whatsoever thy hand findeth to do, do it with thy might; for there is no work, nor device, nor knowledge, nor wisdom, in the grave, whither thou goest,*

11 *I returned, and saw under the sun, that the race is not to the swift, nor the battle to the strong, neither yet bread to the wise, nor yet riches to men of understanding, nor yet favour to men of skill; but time and chance happeneth to them all.*

He gave you the chance/opportunity and the way forward to make wealth, either by your labour or through an inheritance left behind by your parents. You are to be passionate and remember the vulnerable groups or individual within your environment to care and show them love as your Creator (God) is Love. You have to emulate your Heavenly Father because it is a privilege, not a right, to be created in the likeness of God. He would have made you and me to be something else *(Genesis 1:26, 27)*

26 *And God said, Let us make man in our image, after our likeness: and let them have dominion over the fish of the sea, and over the fowl of the air, and over the cattle, and over all the earth, and over every thing that creepeth upon the earth.*

27 *So God created man in his own image, in the image of God created he him; male and female created he them.*

Nonetheless, this is an awakening piece of manuscript, especially after this terrible pandemic, in which the entire world has been affected in one capacity or another. It is applicable to everyone, no matter your colour or background. Also, for the entire world to acknowledge that God owns the Universe and is in control. He does as HE pleases. The virus went round the globe. It has no respect for gender, creed, religion or your economic status. Humanity should endeavour to fear their Creator God, and abstain from sins or hatred that displeases Him.

In summary you are created to have a good relationship with God and humanity because God is relational. Also, to impact your world, to make a huge difference to your generation, thereby leaving a good legacy during your time and not as the unproductive fig tree, gaining ground with vain results.

Therefore, caring is the sharing that lies in giving, loving, advocating, sponsorship etc, as it is advisable for you and me to be problem solvers to someone in need. You are created with nothing and you exit with nothing. The empty chamber from the ephemeral thing that portrayed the frailty of mankind signalled you are existing via borrowed time and chance. At the end of human existence, all positions, wealth, power and material goods acquired are vanity. May you and I be counted worthy towards the Heavenly Kingdom and be blessed as you read this awakening book.

The Borrowed Space (Part I) Applicable to the Ephemeral Thing

———◁◇▷———

Jesus Christ of Nazareth is our role model. He made a drastic impact on humanity. He was conceived via a borrowed womb, and even during delivery, there was no space at the inn, like a maternity ward in a hospital, but he was born among sheep in a manger. He lived a lonely life as a servant, yet He was the Master, He was not educated but referred to as the Rabbi, the Teacher, the great Physician, the Healer of all manner of sickness during his earthly ministration. His accusers were among the people He fed, delivered, healed, blessed, and did all manner of good towards, yet he was crucified on the Cross of Calvary. He was even buried in a borrowed tomb.

The basic foundation of a typical example of a ***borrowed space partway*** is via Jesus Christ of Nazareth the Son of the Virgin Mary, from conception, through delivery, towards His ministerial life before crucifixion and burial in a borrowed grave. He lived a lonely but humble lifestyle, one for humanity to emulate.

Jesus Christ of Nazareth is teaching us that whatever we have, or however wealthy, you and I are being borrowed for our effective daily living. Your riches or wealth does not belongs to you alone. HE is teaching humanity to learn to share and care for one another.

The Angel Gabriel visited the mother of Lord Jesus Christ with a prophesy about how highly favoured she was, and how she would conceive and give birth with a signified name through a ***borrowed womb*** which was against the normal custom before traditional marriage ***(Luke 1: 26-38).***

26   ***And in the sixth month the angel Gabriel was sent from God unto a city of Galilee, named Nazareth.***

27 *To a virgin espoused to a man whose name was Joseph, of the house of David; and the virgin's name was Mary.*

28 *And the angel came in unto her, and said, Hail, thou that art highly favoured, the Lord is with thee: blessed art thou among women.*

29 *And when she saw him, she was troubled at his saying, and cast in her mind what manner of salutation this should be.*

30 *And the angel said unto her, fear not, Mary: for thou hast found favour with God.*

31 *And, behold, thou shalt conceive in the womb, and bring forth a son, and shalt call his name JESUS.*

32 *He shall be great, and shall be called the Son of the Highest: and the Lord God shall give unto him the throne of his father David:*

33 And he shall reign over the house of Jacob for ever; and of his kingdom there shall be no end.

34 Then said Mary unto the angel, How shall this be, seeing I know not a man?

35 And the angel answered and said unto her, the Holy Ghost shall come upon thee, and the power of the Highest shall overshadow thee therefore also that holy thing which shall be born of thee shall be called the Son of God.

36 And, behold, thy cousin Elisabeth she hath also conceived a son in her old age: and this is the sixth month with her, who was called barren.

37 For with God nothing shall be impossible.

38 And Mary said, Behold the handmaid of the Lord; be it unto me according to thy word. And the angel departed from her.

The above information was a prophetic instruction, which is very scary. Can you relate it to your routine lifestyle if your future partner came up with the notion of the situation Mary found herself in? It would have resulted in a sort of humiliation. The question is, how righteous or faithful are you and I towards God or our neighbour? Can you be a good custodian of positivity? Mary was not the only girl within her community at that time but she obtained favour from above to be the vessel God will use to birth the Saviour of the World. May you and I be preferred in the agenda of the Almighty God.

Thereafter, Joseph had an encounter with God via an angelic visitation through the dream not to put Mary away. She would have been stoned to death according to their custom *(Matthew 1:18-25)*

18 *Now the birth of Jesus Christ was on this wise: When as his mother Mary was espoused to Joseph, before they came together, she was found with child of the Holy Ghost.*

19 *Then Joseph her husband, being a just man, and not willing to make her a public example, was minded to put her away privily.*

20 *But while he thought on these things, behold, the angel of the Lord appeared unto him in a dream, saying, Joseph, thou son of David, fear not to take unto thee Mary thy wife: for that which is conceived in her is of the Holy Ghost.*

21 *And she shall bring forth a son, and thou shalt call his name JESUS: for he shall save his people from their sins.*

22 *Now all this was done, that it might be fulfilled which was spoken of the Lord by the prophet, saying,*

23 *Behold, a virgin shall be with child, and shall bring forth a son, and they shall call his name Emmanuel, which being interpreted is, God with us.*

24 *Then Joseph being raised from sleep did as the angel of the Lord had bidden him, and took unto him his wife.*

25 *And knew her not till she had brought forth her firstborn son: and he called his name JESUS.*

Joseph adhered to the instruction of the angel. In one capacity or another, the Lord must have ministered to you. Are you law-abiding, does your character demonstrate an obedient son/daughter of God? Please remember obedience was the first Law in heaven. It was when Adam and Eve disobeyed at the Garden of Eden that the whole plan of God towards mankind was destabilised and reformed.

Furthermore, during the birth of Baby Jesus Christ of Nazareth there was no space at the Inn, similar to the Maternity Hospital and its labour wards in our time. It was fully booked, so Jesus was given birth to in a ***manger, a borrowed space*** where sheep were reared. No wonder the Psalmist stated in ***(Psalms 23:1)***

The LORD is my Shepherd, I shall not want...

The Saviour of the Universe had no place to be cared for during his earthly birth, but the Almighty God was in the midst of that situation. Jesus Christ of Nazareth went through what you are going through to be interceding on your behalf in the presence of God.

Hence, when He is with you, He never fails.

The Lord was the main focus. HE is our sources, our basic needs supplier and where good tidings originated from. We shall not want for anything good as long as we trust and lean on Him.

The Borrowed Space (Part II)

During Jesus' Ministerial Outreach He was showcased publicly with miracles, signs and wonders whereby He stepped into diverse circumstances to save and deliver healing for all manner of sickness. You are also created to intercede, advocate, to do something to help others. They were invited to a marriage ceremony whereby His mother would not have anxiously persuaded Him to step into the ugly situation to avert shame among the family gathering at Canaan of Galilee when the wine was running out. The mother knew what her son could do from her experience at home, but kept it to herself. Mary drew His attention to address the need of wine, and He initially responded:

Jesus saith unto her, Woman, what have I to do with thee? Mine hour is not yet come (John 2:4). for he knew what was ahead of him.

The mother never took offence but instead gave instruction: ***His mother saith unto the servants, Whatsoever he saith unto you, do it (John 2: 5).***

Jesus Christ responded to the concerns: ***water pots were borrowed*** and the Sovereignty power of the Lord manifested. The new wine was better than the former produced by the host. May our later end on this planet be meaningful as we adhere to the obedience of God. The Lord manifested His power and shame was averted. May we not be put to shame on the day of our celebrations. May the Lord send us helpers of destiny in Jesus Mighty Name Amen.

Furthermore, during His ministrations when He was about to preach, He ***borrowed Simon's Boat***, ***the Platform to*** preach his earthly ministration ***(Luke 5: 1-3)***

And it came to pass, that as the people pressed upon him to hear the word of God, he stood by the lake of Gennesaret.

2   And saw two ships standing by the lake:

but the fishermen were gone out of them, and were washing their nets.

3   *And he entered into one of the ships, which was Simon's, and prayed him that he would thrust out a little from the land. And he sat down, and taught the people out of the ship.*

Simon was frustrated and expressed his feelings after much struggle all through the night. When he complained to Jesus, he had no option but to adhere to Jesus Christ's instruction:

Verse 4 Now when he had left speaking, he said unto Simon, Launch out into the deep, and let down your nets for a draught.

5   *And Simon answering said unto him, Master, we have toiled all the night, and have taken nothing: nevertheless, at thy word I will let down the net.*

In obedience to the Lord's word as he stated, nevertheless, in accordance to your word, he launched into the deep and caught multitudes.

Have you ever been in a business and faced

with challenges or disappointments? The key solution is for you and me to take it to the Lord in prayer. He will do it for you; He has done it before. In obedience, and believe He is able, no matter the situation, delay is not denial of that good plan of God towards your fulfilment.

Simon Peter toiled all the night but caught nothing. Thanks to his obedience, his character and his passion towards the outreach in preaching the word of God, he released his boat at that particular time, although filled with disappointment and frustration. His intention was to put food on the family's table and pay his bills, but his obedience earned him a positive outcome and endless joy. He had more than enough and became one of the Apostles of Jesus. At the end Apostle Peter assisted Jesus first before he obtained the blessing. There is a great reward in your giving either your money, time, space etc.

Furthermore, Jesus ministered at a point in time drawing near towards evening He did not want to send the crowd away hungry or fainting on their way to their various homes. He made a demand for food, but one of the disciples realised that in the midst of crowd there was a lad amongst the multitude with packed lunch of two fishes and five loaves of bread.

Jesus borrowed a packed lunch (John 6: 4-13).

And the Passover, a feast of the Jews, was nigh.

5   *When Jesus then lifted up his eyes , and saw a great company come unto him, he saith unto Philip, Whence shall we buy bread, that these may eat?*

6   *And this he said to prove him: for he himself knew what he would do.*

7   *Philip answered him, two hundred pennyworth of bread is not sufficient for them, that every one of them may take a little.*

8   *One of the disciples, Andrew, Simon Peter's brother, saith unto him,*

9   *There is a lad here, which hath five barley loaves, and two small fishes: but what are they among so many?*

10   And Jesus said, Make the men sit down. Now there was much grass in the place. So the men sat down, in number about five thousand.

11   And Jesus took the loaves; and when he had given thanks, he distributed to the disciples, and disciples to them that were sat down; and likewise of the fishes as much as they would.

12   When they were filled, he said unto his disciples, Gather up the fragments that remain, nothing be loss.

13   Therefore they gathered them together, and filled twelve basket with the fragments of the five barley loaves, which remained over and above unto them that had eaten.

As He gave instructions the food was multiplied and twelve baskets were left over. **They had more than enough**. The young lad was blessed because he had compassion towards people. As advisable by Apostle Paul from the book of *(Act 20:35):*

I have shewed you all things, how that so labouring ye ought to support the weak, and to remember the words of the Lord Jesus, how he said, It is more blessed to give than to receive.

He encouraged his brethren as stated above, though it was the only quotation from Jesus Christ that was not recorded in the Gospels because Paul had a spiritual encounter with Jesus Christ. The young lad gave his little packed lunch, and had overflowing food in return. The same is applicable to you; whenever you do good, surely there is a great reward.

Also, from the account of ***(John 3:16):***

For God so loved the world, that he gave his only begotten Son, that whosoever believeth in him should not perish, but have everlasting life.

God loved His creation and gave all to save humanity by releasing his only Son. The question is, what have you been given to impact your world? God has given everyone on earth one gift or skill to serve humanity. Whatever you perceived belongs to you, it is just for a while (Ephemeral thing). You do not own it but to be someone's helper of destiny. Thus: are you giving to a good cause.

During Jesus' triumphant entry into Jerusalem, He had no vehicles nor donkey to ride but made a demand for His disciples to go into the village to **untie the Colt (borrowed transportation).** He instructed that if anyone asked questions, the response was that the Lord was in need of it *(Mark 11: 1-3).*

And when they came nigh to Jerusalem, unto Bethphage and Bethany, at the mount of Olives, he sendeth forth two of his disciples,

2 *And saith unto them, Go your way into the village over against you: and as soon as ye be entered into it, ye shall find a colt tied, wherein never man sat; loose him, and bring him.*

3 *And if any man say unto you, Why do ye this? Say ye that the Lord hath need of him; and straightaway he will send him hither.*

You and I originated from a particular place of birth but from a diverse family. Do you realise that the Lord is in need of you? You are created in His image for a purpose *(Genesis 1: 26-27)*,

And God said, Let us make man in our image, after our likeness: and let them have dominion over the fish of the sea, and over the fowl of the air, and over the cattle and over all the earth, and over everything that creepeth upon the earth.

27 *So God created man in his own image, in the image of God created he him; male and female created he them.*

You are here on earth for a purpose; to make an impact on your world. You are created to make a positive influence on yourself, your family, your community and at a global level. You are not here by mistake but to make a difference to humanity, no matter what your background, colour, creed or gender. God is interested in you and me. God has a better plan for your life. The colt that was tied was released at the appointed time for a significant assignment and shown off with shouts of acclamation: "Hallelujah to the Highest!" These were the voices of joyful celebration.

When you are in your place of assignment, you will be happy and fulfilled. God Himself will be pleased with you as an obedient servant who adhered to His commandment. The colt was held captive until Jesus untied it for a purpose. Wherever you may have lost hope, as the colt was untied to fulfilled divine assignment, may you and myself be untied to fulfil divine purpose in life in Jesus Mighty Name Amen. Jesus Christ is the helper of the helpless has a better plan for you, HE will aid you and me in all distress Amen.

In a later state towards the end of Jesus' earthly ministry, He instructed His disciples that they needed a space for the "Lord's Supper" that was performed in a ***borrowed upper room (Mark 14: 12-17)***

And the first day of unleavened bread, when they killed the passover, his disciples said unto him, Where wilt thou that we go and prepare that thou mayest eat the passover?

13   And he sendeth forth two of his disciples, and saith unto them, Go ye into the city, and there shall meet you a man bearing a pitcher of water: follow him.

14   And wheresoever he shall go in, say ye to the goodman of the house, The Master saith, Where I shall eat the Passover with my disciples?

15   And he will shew you a large upper room furnished and prepared: there make ready for us.

16   And his disciples went forth, and came into the city, and found as he had said unto them; and they made ready the Passover.

17   And in the evening he cometh with the twelve.

All the above illustration was signposting the fact that the Creator of the universe is a typical example of what is being demonstrated in this Book as an Ephemeral Thing, and how vulnerable an organ is without the means of breathing that makes the system to become an Empty Chamber. At the end of this journey, life is not worth unnecessary stress. If the Saviour of the world could be so humbled from conception till his exit on earth, then why holden to materialism with short time limits? It seems like a vapour of no recognition in a later state.

It was after the last supper that there came the beginning of his betrayal through one of his disciples, Judas Iscariot. Thereafter, He was arrested, suffered and crucified. Simon the Cyrene helped Jesus to carry His Cross before He was crucified *(Matthew 27: 32).*

And as they came out, they found a man of Cyrene, Simon by name: him they compelled to bear his cross.

He was compelled to support the agony towards Calvary and was buried in a **borrowed tomb** owned by Joseph of Arimathaea, one of His secret disciples. He allowed Jesus Christ of Nazareth's body to be buried in the grave purchased for himself *(Matthew 27: 57-60)*

When the even was come, there came a rich man of Arimathaea, named Joseph, who also himself was Jesus disciple:

58   He went to Pilate, and begged the body of Jesus. Then Pilate commanded the body to be delivered.

59 And when Joseph had taken the body, he wrapped it in a clean linen cloth,

60 And laid it in his own new tomb, which he had hewn out in the rock: and he rolled a great stone to the door of the sepulchre, and departed.

What a privilege to be counted worthy of the provider of the resting place for the Saviour of the World. Nevertheless, Jesus Christ of Nazareth is our role model and He is risen.

Jesus Christ, the same yesterday, and today, and forever (Hebrew 13: 8).

He reigns forever. HE Is alive!

All the mentioned examples is for our learning not to hold unto vain glory. It's just for a shot period (Ephemeral Thing), because as the breathing is seized, the chamber becomes empty and inactive, and the regulating system stops. It is only the legacy left behind that will speak for you. The Master of the Universe came to this world to be a typical example to emulate. Please don't get me wrong, it is good to be wealthy, but the focus is to be someone who is a helper of destiny. Jesus was assisted all through His life.

So also, you and I need to portray our Mentor's lifestyle. No matter the materialistic acquired is_just for a short time. The needful thing is to show kindness and be good towards one another because at the end of the Earthly race it is Vanity. You brought nothing and exit with naught.

RIGHTEOUS LIFESTYLES

To live a righteous pathway is to abide by the principles and commandments of God. In the secular realm, it is to abide to laid-down rules and regulations or policies to be a law-abiding citizen. As God's creation, Love what He says He loved and hate what displeases Him. Due to the major wants of humanity, like struggling for power, money, materialism etc., many people never come to the realization that the Covid-19 pandemic has been an awakening for humanity. It is for the entire universe to sit back, reflect and examine what lifestyles are applicable to healthy living. You try as much as possible to live a life that pleases God, to do what is needful to humanity. If you don't want people to hurt you, please don't try it on others.

Remember that the entire world was created by only one God, the supernatural unseen Guest who watches over His handiwork. The Nations of the Earth are ruled by Him. No matter your colour, nationality, race, gender or background, you are the seed of Abraham. He was a man referred to as a righteous man due to his believe and obedience to God's commandment *(Genesis 15: 1-6)*:

After these things the word of the LORD came unto Abram in a vision, saying Fear not, Abram: I am thy shield, and thy exceeding great reward.

2   *And Abram said, LORD GOD, what wilt thou give me, seeing I go childless, and the steward of my house is this Eliezer of Damascus?*

3   *And Abram said: Behold, to me thou hast given no seed: and, lo, one born in my house is my heir.*

4   *And, behold, the word of the LORD came unto him, saying, This shall not be thine heir; but he that shall come forth out of thine own bowels shall be thine heir.*

5 *And he brought him forth abroad, and said, Look now toward heaven, and tell the stars, if thou be able to number them: and he said unto him, So shall thy seed be.*

6 *And he believed in the LORD: and he counted it to him for righteousness.*

Have you been instructed to do anything and still doubting? Do not fear, because He who sent you will back you up in all your endeavours. Please note that delayed obedience is a disobedience resulting in unbelieving and unrighteousness. You are created to worship God and to impact people's lives. Your wealth is to make a difference to people's lives. We all have an important role to play towards one another. I need you to survive, the same applicable to you. You are created in the image of God. The head cannot tell the eyes that I do not need your help or assistance. The mouth cannot do without the hand, nor the leg. They all have different job descriptions. The question is, why is there hatred all over the universe? The Lord dislikes this (***Proverb 6 16-19):***

These six things doth the LORD hate: yea, seven are an abomination unto him:

17   Haughty eyes, a lying tongue, and hands that shed innocent blood,

18   An heart that deviseth wicked imaginations, feet that be swift in running to mischief,

19   A false witness that speaketh lies, and he that soweth discord among brethren.

The above were seven abominations the Lord hates. He despises these negative behaviours and personalities. People are maltreating the handiwork of God through killing, not only by stabbing or the use of guns but also through the small element (tongues). They are doing all sorts of ill acts towards their fellow human beings. Please may I suggest that it is now time for you as an individual to change, if you consider your way of life is not in the right pathway.

On that note, the unpleasant actions that portray hatred, unrest, war or other negative lifestyles should stop, because there is no point in killing one another for vain glory, something that is in temporary utilization in this earthly realm. All the struggles of this world end in vanity. It is not worth unnecessary pressure because is for an ephemeral thing –temporary ownership. One day you will exit from this earthly platform and give an account of your life to your Creator. Will it be of good reward or otherwise? Strive to live a righteous life that is pleasing unto God. Let's makes our Heavenly Father happy and consider our attitude towards humanity to obtain His approval, for all worldly affairs will be seized someday because you are only a sojourner, on a pilgrimage.

MATERIALISTIC LIFESTYLES

There are various instances of materialistic lifestyles, but I will mention one or two from the Word of God for our learning, such as Lot's wife and Ananias and Sapphira.

Lot, who was Abraham's nephew, and his family were visited by an angel and told to flee from their environment because the wrath of God was about to destroy the city *(Genesis 19: 15-26)*;

And when the morning arose, the angels hastened Lot, saying Arise, take thy wife, and thy two daughters which are here lest thou be consumed in the iniquity of the city.

16 And while he lingered, the men laid hold upon his hand, and upon the hand of his wife, and upon the hand of his two daughters; the LORD being merciful unto him: and they brought him forth, and set him without the city.

17 *And it came to pass, when they had brought them forth abroad, that he said, Escape for thy life; look not behind thee, neither stay thou in all the plain; escape to the mountain, lest thou be consumed.*

18 *And Lot said unto them, Oh, not so my Lord:*

19 *Behold now, thy servant hath found grace in thy sight, and thou hast magnified thy mercy, which thou hast shewed unto me in saving my life; and I cannot escape to the mountain, lest some evil take me, and I die:*

20 *Behold now, this city is near to flee unto, and it is a little one: Oh let me escape thither, (is it not a little one?) and my soul shall live.*

21 *And he said unto him, See, I have accepted thee concerning this thing*

also, that I will not overthrow this city, for them which thou hast spoken.

22   *Haste thee, escape thither; for I cannot do anything till thou become thither; Therefore the name of the city was called Zoar.*

23   *The sum was risen upon the earth when Lot entered into Zoar.*

24   *Then the LORD rained upon Sodom and upon Gomorrah brimstone and fire from the LORD out of heaven.*

25   *And he overthrew those cities, and all the plain, and all the inhabitants of the cities, and that which grew upon the ground.*

26   *But his wife looked back from behind him, and she became a pillar of salt.*

The above passage illustrated the fact that Lot was a righteous man and his spirit was always vexed by the unlawful deeds of his Sodomite neighbours, so doubtless he will encounter challenges. When you are amongst people of negative influence or personality, in one way or the other you will be affected. Jesus used this incident as a warning for us not to look back. When there is an instruction, prompt action needs to be in place.

Lot's wife apparently lingered behind, continually and longingly looking back on her beloved possessions, and was buried by the explosion that resulted from the destruction of the city while she became a pillar of salt. Materialistic lifestyles dominated her thinking faculty, then wasted her precious soul. She had forgotten that when she was alive, whatever she had lost during the escape from the city could be regained. When there is life, there is still hope. Nonetheless, every possession on this planet is an ephemeral thing.

Let's ponder on another incident concerning a couple who lied against the power of the Holy Spirit that fetched them out. Nobody advocated for them to render their properties in a deceitful way. That teaching is for our learning. If you deceived man, you cannot deceive God. It was the Lord Himself at work through the disciples. Therefore, you need to obey God and His commandment and go by the rule or laid-down policy either in the community, nation, churches, mosques even at the market place. When Jesus was asked to pay tax, He commanded Peter to fetch fish and paid. He asked him what was in the money, and Peter responded that it was the head of Caesar. Jesus advised him "Give unto Caesar what is due to Caesar and unto God what belongs to God". Be law abiding and let your light shine amongst men. Be a positive role model, because you are the Epistle the world is reading.

Their character, attitude and lifestyles within themselves are of not telling the truth about their possessions for giving aid. This is a voluntary action, not compulsory, but an intention to show off within the congregation of how wealthy they are, thereby intimidating other fellow brethren who could not afford one meal on their table on the proceeds of a deceitful act. They are unaware that it was God that was in control, and thereby the Holy Spirit terminated their ill act and were destroyed. This incident is to teach us not to act ludicrously.

(Act 5:1-11)

But a certain man named Ananias, with Sapphira his wife sold a possession.

2   *And kept back part of the price, his wife also being privy to it, and brought a certain part, and laid it at the apostle's feet.*

3   *But Peter said, Ananias, why hath Satan filled thine heart to lie to the Holy Ghost, and to keep back part of the price of the land?*

4   *While it remained, was it not thine own? And after it was sold, was it not in thine own power? Why hast thou conceived this thing in thine heart? Thou hast not lied unto men, but unto God.*

5   *And Ananias hearing these words fell down, and gave up the ghost: and great fear came on all them that heard these things.*

6   *And the young men arose, wound him up, and carried him out, and buried him.*

7 *And it was about the space of three hours after, when his wife, not knowing what was done, came in.*

8 *And Peter answered unto her, Tell me whether ye sold the land for so much? And she said, Yea, for so much.*

9 *Then Peter said unto her, How is it that ye have agreed together to tempt the Spirit of the Lord? behold, the feet of them which have buried thy husband are at the door, and shall carry thee out.*

10 *Then fell she down straightway at his feet, and yielded up the ghost: and the young men came in, and found her dead, and, carrying her forth, buried her by her husband.*

11 *And great fear came upon all the church, and upon as many as heard these things.*

This signifies that you do not need to lie for material gain, nor for recognition nor to obtained any approval from humanity, with the only exception of God. Whatever you do to the next person is unto God, and He who sees in secret will reward you openly. This couple portrayed a negative role model for their family, mostly their children and generations unborn. The pandemic signals uniqueness and oneness, and to love one another globally. It is for the individual to have that motive of team spirit and passion but not an accumulating wealth mind set nor a selfish interest. You brought nothing and exit with naught.

MATERIALISTIC LIFESTYLES

There are many instances, but I will mention one or two as we bring it to our journey of life for our learning. Many lives have been destabilised due to conspiracy, lies, betrayal of thrust etc. The issue is: ***why do the heathen rage, and the people imagine a vain thing? (Psalm 2:1)***

a) From the book of Genesis Chapter 42 (but focused on 45:1-7), as Joseph's brethren conspired against him and in the end sold him into slavery because of his dream.

Then Joseph could not refrain himself before all them that stood by him; and he cried, Cause every man to go out from me. And there stood no man with him, while Joseph made himself known unto his brethren.

2   *And he wept aloud: and the Egyptians and the house of Pharaoh heard.*

3   *And Joseph said unto his brethren, I am Joseph; doth my father yet live? And his brethren could not answer him; for they were troubled at his presence.*

4   *And Joseph said unto his brethren, Come near to me, I pray you. And they came near. And he said, I am Joseph your brother, whom ye sold into Egypt.*

5   *Now therefore be not grieved, nor angry with yourselves, that ye sold me hither: for God did send me before you to preserve life.*

6   *For these two years hath the famine been in the land: and yet there are five years, in the which there shall neither be earing nor harvest.*

7   *And God sent me before you to preserve you a posterity in the earth, and to save your lives by a great deliverance.*

There are some vision killers like Joseph's brethren. Dear readers, please kindly consider your ways among your brethren, family, colleagues at work or business partners. It could be within the church group or mosques or in the market places. On that note, if you have in one way or another conspired against someone, which is not acceptable in God's principles, He hates that. Nevertheless, despite all odds, destiny cannot be changed. Joseph was sold into slavery, imprisoned and held back, but God proved His Sovereignty power at the end of his journey. Therefore, no matter what you are going through, may I suggest to you, let your hand be clean, and the great advocator will vindicate you. God is just, and there is no unrighteousness in him.

At the end, Joseph's dream came to manifestation. He was honoured in the presence of his cruel brethren. No matter what challenges you have experienced or might be going through, rest assured that God is there with you, and regardless of what you might be going through it is temporal because everything is just for a season. From the account of *(Job 14:1-2);*

1) ***Man that is born of a woman is of few days, and full of trouble.***

2) ***He cometh forth like a flower, and is cut down: he fleeth also as a shadow, and continueth not.***

The passage demonstrates how frail humanity is. Hence come to the realization that you are a stranger on a journey. Did you know when the oxygen is seized within the system the person will be declared passed on – thus the last office that signals emptiness? So also, this empty chamber, now portrayed in worldly affairs as an ephemeral thing.

Therefore, this is an awakening book that emphasises the opportunity of sparing individual lives after the horrible pandemic, a deadly global virus that despised integrity and status. Remember you are born to dominate in accordance to God's agenda. To attain that great reward is for you and me to keep His commandment, To Love your neighbour as yourself, and help those in needs for your assistant. You are created to impact your world and to make a different not only to be wealthy for self-centredness. May you and myself be a good vessel unto honour for the Master's use in Jesus Name Amen.

b) The woman caught in adultery: the scribes and the Pharisees conspired against her while they reported the incident to Jesus *(John 8:1-11)*:

1   *Jesus went unto the mount of Olives.*

2   *And early in the morning he came again into the temple, and all the people came unto him; and he sat down, and taught them.*

3   *And the scribes and Pharisees brought unto him a woman taken in adultery; and when they had set her in the midst,*

4   *They say unto him, Master, this woman was taken in adultery, in the very act.*

5   *Now Moses in the law commanded us, that such should be stoned: but what sayest thou?*

6   *This they said, tempting him, that they might have to accuse him. But Jesus*

stooped down, and with his finger wrote on the ground, as though he heard them not.

7   *So when they continued asking him, He that is without sin among you, let him first cast a stone at her.*

8   *And again he stooped down, and wrote on the ground.*

9   *And they which heard it, being convicted by their own conscience, went out one by one, beginning at the eldest, even unto the last: and Jesus was left alone, and the woman standing in the midst.*

10   *When Jesus had lifted up himself, and saw none but the woman, he said unto her, Woman, where are those thine accusers? Hath no man condemned thee?*

11   *She said, No man, Lord. And Jesus said unto her, Neither do I condemn thee: go, sin no more.*

The above example was a sinful act that demanded stoning to death according to the

Mosaic law which was addressed by Jesus Christ, the great advocate, and she was set free. The world is full of hypocritical lifestyles. Thank God, for His mercies endured forever. You don't defile the temple of the Lord, for you are created in His image. However, it takes two to tango. They conspired against the woman, but what happened to the man? It took the grace of God to intercede on behalf of the woman, otherwise she would have been killed. There are instances when you need to stand in the gap, to save someone in danger, to advocate on behalf of somebody. By your little support you are impacting lives and God loves that. Whenever you need attention surely God will raise helpers to come to your aid.

May the mercies of the Lord that prevailed over judgement speak as occasion demands for you and me through our journey of life. Please strive as much as possible to live a life that is pleasing unto the Lord and to be a positive role model.

Theatre Encounter

✦

As a student nurse, before you complete your programme of training, there are various stages to go through. You undergo some basic placement, which is mandatory, before branching off into a designated area or speciality of interest. When you see a person conveyed to the theatre on the stretcher, there are preparations to be made before any surgery taken place. The nurse has to get the patient ready for the theatre. Then the anaesthetist carries out his role of sedating the patient, or putting the patient to sleep, before the surgeon can start carrying out the procedure. Seeing humanity on that surgical table, the patient has no clue what will come next. He or she is vulnerable, agitated, even anxious, until fully put to sleep and in a state of unconsciousness.

My first experience was a procedure for a total knee replacement. It was then that I realised that when people are healthy, no one realises or appreciates the handiwork of nature orchestrated by our Creator, The Almighty God. During my placement, to taste or partake of food with blood, even beef, was very challenging. It seemed I was in a different world entirely. It took a while for me to readjust. Then I realised that it's our breathing and the circulatory system that make us human – nothing else. You have no Idea what the surgeon is doing, or the medical team. It was a speciality department that I hugely appreciated in the hospital.

Let's ponder on this case study: A baby delivered within the hospital's maternity unit. He/she cannot be delivered with money, ornaments, nor clothing. In case you have seen one it will result in a huge controversial scenario termed as abnormality. The same is applicable when someone dies; he/she goes with nothing. Although there are some cultures and religious organisations that do not use a coffin or casket to bury their loved ones. I perceived that they considered it as a vain state. He/she came with nothing so they will exit with nothing. Please do not forget that at the end of it all the entire world's unrest amounts to nothing. It is not worth disunity or hatred. When the oxygen is stopped within the system, then it becomes an empty chamber, because there is no more of the blood that is routinely pumped through the ventricles of the heart. It was then I realised that we are dignified by God, who bred us. It's our breathing that enhances all activities of daily living.

There are various wards within the hospital environment, like the orthopaedic wards, where a patient, after going through surgery, would be on total dependency for a while. Then you realise that when someone is sick you cannot function, nor are you actively competent for normal duties. On that rests the truth: health is wealth. Your healthiness determines your routine capabilities, while ill health is nothing to wish on anyone, even to be infected with the Covid-19 virus despite a restricted protocol of isolation, social distancing, sanitisation, wearing of masks etc. People cannot have contact with families nor friends. However, some individuals have suffered depression, loneliness etc, an issue of mental health incapacity that needs further investigation and support. The circulatory system is regulated by blood and whenever the oxygen stops it's a critical incident that needs an emergency crash team. I pray that you and I shall not go before our time on earth and that we shall fulfil our divine purpose according to God's plan.

As illustrated by the scriptures, all of man's life is just a short time. Please be aware that this world is not yours but you are just a sojourner, and there is accountability awaiting you and me at the end of this earthly race as you abide by his commandment, and reverence Him because He is relational.

The pandemic is a typical global incident that portrays how frail humanity is with the ephemeral thing which amounts to nothing. In accordance to *(1st Peter 1:24):*

For all flesh is a as grass, and all the glory of man as the flower of grass. The grass withereth, and the flower thereof falleth away.

What is the use of accumulating worldly things which are of no use to your fellow human beings? Your existence is paramount. You were born to rule, to dominate and to fulfil divine purpose. You are on a gold platter of God's creation. You have no option of failing to achieve your assignment on earth. You and I are shining lights for the entire world to emulate. No matter your background, colour, gender, education or status, what will be said of you is whether your life has been productive or unproductive, like the fig tree gaining ground for nothing.

Hence, the hospital environment is an atmosphere of reflection towards the health and wellness of an individual/family within the community or nation, so talk less of the Covid-19 pandemic which has drastically changed the whole world. Infection control protocols are put in place from patients to health professionals or vice versa. The entire system changed as nations were living by the day and portrayed the essence of living in a healthy environment, as you don't know if you have ever been infected by the virus. Unpredictable statistics are sickening, and make you realise that this world is neither yours nor mine. Let's see in the next chapter how it demonstrates the sides effects of the pandemic.

THE POSITIVE AND NEGATIVE IMPACTS OF THE PANDEMIC

There are always two sides to every situation, including that of the pandemic. This will be mentioned briefly because everyone knew that even the little children were restricted and told to compulsorily wear masks. Key workers such as health professionals, government employees who were involved in face-to-face contact with the general public, train and bus drivers, teachers were given priority for shopping. The same applied to the vulnerable and elderly groups who were fully supported, like Meals on Wheels, they were assisted with shopping, and carers were put in place. The homeless were looked after as local housing authorities took it on board to move vulnerable groups off the streets. There were tremendous humanitarian influences, while comparison and human elements were put aside.

Health and well-being was the top priority of global concerns as research made accelerated progress towards the development of vaccines to address the deadly virus. Covid-19 was a global issue requiring immediate attention. It was a global instruction that all places of worship had to have restricted access. Leisure centres, cinema, pubs, etc were closed to avoid the spreading of the deadly virus. Some people affected by the lockdown policy during the pandemic developed creative skills. Instead of being idle they spent their time inventing or creating something. It was a time to be innovative and to reflect. Some groups of people took the opportunity to develop new careers, saving money to buy a home, or investing in a business venture.

Along the line many organisations laid off their workers and made them redundant, and some individuals, due to losing their jobs, developed conditions that impaired their health and wellness, like loneliness, depression or low self-esteem, or adopted negative lifestyles and became drug addicts or developed eating disorders etc. Poverty was widespread due to lack of sources of income or livelihood. Families and friends separated because of the need for isolation, to avoid cross-infection, and social distancing and restriction of movement were enforced. Some children, due to financial constraints, had no access to PC facilities; they missed out on routine studies and lectures via e-learning on Zoom. These were very challenging circumstances, because children with learning disabilities and language barriers need extra support. Nonetheless, various boroughs were able to do as much as they could to support their community. The elderly, refugees, unemployed or people on furlough schemes were signposted to diverse charity supporting groups. There were collaborations between partners to ensure none was left behind during the pandemic.

Some parents were able to spend time at home with their children but had no opportunity for a normal annual family holiday, either at home or abroad. There was no air travel, as everywhere was locked down. Also, some professionals took the opportunity to work from home while some had to actively execute their daily work by travelling with reduced transportation facilities as regulated by TFL (Transport for London), either by bus, train, underground or tram. It was a very challenging period with little face-to-face contact.

Nonetheless, there were fewer incidents of crime, as every individual was on guard protecting their lives. Drastic precautions were in place because the virus was very contagious, while globally health took the highest priority to save lives. There were so many diverse posters, with detailed information and signposted instructions for people to know what they needed to know, what to do and where to avoid such as 'Stay home and save lives'. The news was the order of the day 24/7, with horrible statistics. The notion was that as people adhered to the precautions individual were made to keep fellow citizens and brethren safe.

The most critical aspect of this was that bereaved families were unable to bid their loved ones who had died farewell, as all protocol towards Covid-19 needed to be adhered to. Dignitaries with reputable status passed unto glory during the pandemic and it meant nothing but vanity.

Nevertheless, people never came to the realization that the pandemic was an awakening call to humanity. It is for the entire world to sit back and reflect. Thus, try as much as possible to do the needful and what is right for your neighbour and for humanity. What you don't want people to do to you, don't try it on others. I need you to survive and vice versa. You are created in the image of God. The head cannot dictate to the eyes 'I do not need you', nor can the mouth do without the hand or the leg. The body parts have various job descriptions. The pandemic has shown that no man is an island; we are all one to the controller of the universe, who is our Creator. We are the seed of Abraham. He was a man whom God referred to as a righteous man. He lived a life pleasing unto God. Remember, that the entire world was created by one God. The nations of the earth are governed and controlled by Him.

At the end, with God's divine intervention, the universe had no clue what next step to take rather than interceding in a global prayer forum all over the world. It was then that the medical experts' joint efforts yielded a positive outcome with the wisdom, knowledge, understanding and technical know-how to go about inventing the vaccines that were produced. The administration of the Covid-19 vaccination has now curbed or subdued this dreadful killer virus.

The continuity of sharing and caring for one another is the most important key towards the positive outcome of the pandemic. Covid-19 brought the entire world together. When you love, you will not hate nor do evil to yourself nor to another. Love is a commandment and mandatory from our Creator. God is relational. The pandemic enhanced togetherness, sharing and caring for one another; let us all strive towards the continuity of Love.

Love/Showing Kindness

There are diverse means of showing that you care, such as a few minutes of saying hello, or making a quick phone call. It signifies that you care, and it goes a long way to helping someone out there, most especially within our environment, busy with tight schedules for both young and old. No one is exceptional in touching lives, advocating or interceding on behalf of someone. This should be an action of routine practice, not just a one-off, because the pandemic has built a community spirit within the country, both at local and national level. There are so many charity organisations that took it on board, like the Salvation Army, The Samaritans, The Red Cross etc. Please rest assured that life is relational. The way you treat the next person is paramount in the sight of God because, whatsoever you do to the least of your brother/sister (your neighbour), that is what you do unto God Himself. May I suggest it is advisable to be a good Samaritan (someone helper of destiny). From the account of *(Luke 10:25-37):*

And behold, a certain lawyer stood up, and tempted him, saying, Master, what shall I do to inherit eternal life?

26   *He said unto him, What is written in the law? How readest thou?*

27   *And he answering said, Thou shalt love the Lord thy God with all thy heart, and with all thy soul, and with all thy strength, and with all thy mind; and thy neighbour as thyself.*

28   *And he said unto him, Thou hast answered right: this do, and thou shalt live.*

29   *But he, willing to justify himself, said unto Jesus, And who is my neighbour?*

30   *And Jesus answering said, A certain man went down from Jerusalem to Jericho,*

and fell among thieves, which stripped him of his raiment, ad wounded him, and departed, leaving him half dead.

31 *And by chance there came down certain priest that way: and when he saw him, he passed by on the other side.*

32 *And likewise a Levite; when he was at the place, came and looked on him, and passed by on the other side.*

33 *But a certain Samaritan, as he journeyed, came where he was: and when he saw him, he had compassion on him.*

34 *And went to him, and bound up his wounds, pouring in oil and wine, and set him on his own beast, and brought him to an inn, and took care of him.*

35 *And on the morrow when he departed, he took out two pence, and gave them to the host, and said unto him, Take care of him: and whatsoever thou spendest more, when I come again, I will repay thee.*

36 Which now of these three, thinkest thou, was neighbour unto him that fell among the thieves?

37 And he said, He that shewed mercy on him. Then said Jesus unto him, Go and do thou likewise.

I suggest you and I endeavour to love one another as the Lord commanded, and strive to show kindness as the Good Samaritan did from the above Scripture. Whatsoever you do unto the next person who could be your neighbour is meaningful unto your Creator. Please be aware that all humanity are the seeds of Abraham and as one before the Almighty God. Hence, Love is a commandment he first showed to mankind as he released His Son (*John 3:16*):

For God so loved the world, that he gave his only begotten Son, that whosoever believeth in him should not perish, but have everlasting life.

Someone who cares: because caring is sharing, when you think about others, mostly someone in need or the vulnerable individual or group of people. Relatively, it is the ideology of impacting your world. Your generation needs your attention. No matter what position, power/authority or money anyone has acquired, you are not going from here with it.

There are individuals that took this on board towards a good cause, such as the female Olympic athlete who auctioned her silver medal to help fund heart surgery for a baby a few months old. She was motivated to put her success to good use by auctioning off her medal to help a vulnerable individual that needed support, thereby encouraging the general public by suggestion. In the end, with the help of voluntary funds raised all over, her medal was kept. This was a quote out of passion by this young Olympic athletic: "A medal is only an object, but it can be of great value to others". That is love from within, showing kindness towards a fellow human being.

From times past, we have people like the preacher John Wesley who demonstrated the power of God during revival. Mother Theresa helped the less privileged like feeding the poor

Sir John Major raised a lump sum to support the NHS during the pandemic. Age is not a barrier. The question to you and me is: on what account will your epitaph be inscribed?

Remember all the running up and down and being busy round the clock is termed vanity if it is to no good cause. Please I suggest that you and I endeavour to love one another as the Lord commanded. Try as much as you can to show some kindness.

Conclusion

The rationale behind penning this book is that people have not learned any lessons from the dreadful Covid-19 pandemic. This is a wake-up call to raise the awareness that life is relational, and the way you treat the person next to you is paramount. On that notion of the unpleasant action that people display like hatred, unrest, war and negative lifestyles, there is no point of unrest for vain glory. All the struggles of this world ended in vanity. It is not worth unnecessary pressure, because it only temporary ownership. You do not exit with anything.

Why are negative behaviours raging throughout the entire world, just for materialistic purposes such as money and power? They are all vanity. Nevertheless, I suggest that you and I strive to love one another as the Lord commanded.

I was fortunate enough to be amongst some people who went on a missionary journey to attend a clergy meeting in New York before the news of the dreadful virus, and the statistics were sickening. As indicated above, it will be a critical incident and a dilemma for a new baby delivered with money, nor any ornament or clothing, that will result in a huge, controversial scenario termed an abnormality. So also, if someone has passed on, he or she goes with nothing. He came empty, and he will transit with nothing. Remember all the running up and down and keeping busy round the clock is termed vanity if it is to no good cause.

Note that when there is no oxygen within the organ, it appears empty. It is the air we breathe in that allows us to be acknowledged as a living soul.

The One who owns the universe is demonstrating to us that all opportunities are only for a season. Acquired materialistic wealth, disunity and unrest amount to nothing, but It's only yours for a while. You are here to make a difference – to impact your world. The pandemic made the entire world collaborate and to resolve concerns, which from the scientific perspectives came up with the invention of vaccines to address the issues.

Hence, the empty chamber out of the ephemeral thing that portrays the frailty of mankind, it's a book to raise awareness that you are on a borrowed time and season on earth. As a sojourner you and I must abide by God's commandments, show love to our fellow brethren and strive to utilize our time, talent, wealth, and opportunities to enhance a positive legacy towards our Heavenly home where you will give account how you have traded on this earth full of Vanities. As you are reading it, may you be blessed and achieve the purpose of writing this awakening book.